LIVERPOOL HISTORICAL E!

IRELAND & AMERICA
Their Early Associations, 1500-1640
DAVID B. QUINN

Published for the
DEPARTMENT OF HISTORY
in association with the
INSTITUTE OF IRISH STUDIES
UNIVERSITY OF LIVERPOOL

LIVERPOOL UNIVERSITY PRESS 1991

Liverpool Historical Essays No. 6
General Editor: P.E.H. Hair

First published 1991 by

Liverpool University Press
PO Box 147
Liverpool
L69 3BX

British Library Cataloguing in Publication Data
Data are available
ISBN 0 85323 297 0

Printed by Tudor Print, Bootle, Merseyside

CONTENTS

IRELAND AND AMERICA
1500—1640

I. The Background

In the eighteenth century, Ireland became greatly involved with the emerging society of the North American colonies. Men born in Ireland played a significant part in the American Revolution. Politicians and people in Ireland endeavoured to imitate the Americans in the demand for greater autonomy from England. In the North American case the ocean lent the dissidents the strength to emerge independent, whereas in the Irish case geographical proximity caused dependence to increase to the point of attempted assimilation in a United Kingdom. This is not the history which is told here, but an earlier story: one of surmise at the beginning; of very gradual and slight links and contacts in the sixteenth century; and then the emergence in the early seventeenth century of some part for Ireland to play in the European intervention in the Americas, as colonies developed under the Spanish, Portuguese, French and English. The present account concentrates on North America and the Caribbean islands. The story of Irishmen serving Spain and Portugal elsewhere in the Americas is only touched on.

II. Before Columbus

Ireland has always had a triple orientation, towards Europe, towards Great Britain, and towards the Ocean. At various times the links with Europe or more often with Great Britain have been dominant. The oceanic connection has always been present but has often been of more negative than positive significance. Irishmen have always been sea fishermen and have exploited the food from the seas around their coasts, more especially off their southwest and western shores. It was this seagoing condition which enabled the early Christian hermits to move themselves, in search of solitude and, at times, of pagans to convert, outwards to the north and northwest and perhaps experimentally in other directions. Did Brendan the Bishop in the sixth century explore the sea in the frozen north or even down in the warm and golden south? The tradition that he was a seafarer for part of his life is probably true, but the details of his voyaging belong partly to the Irish tradition of the sea tales (*imrana*), partly to accretions derived from the knowledge of the ninth and later centuries.

Certainly some of the Irish hermits of the early ninth century who went to Iceland returned to pass on knowledge of far northern climes, while Norse settlers in Ireland were later in touch with Greenland as well as Iceland and their tales too may have influenced Brendanian tradition. In respect of the Fortunate Isles (our modern Canaries), searchers for origins for Brendan's discoveries cannot go beyond the classical traditions salvaged by Isidore of Seville not far from the times of Brendan himself. Nor should we forget that those Norsemen who went on from Greenland to Vinland (modern Newfoundland and perhaps other parts of North America) mentioned a Great Ireland which lay near to Vinland and only six days' sailing from Ireland itself. This may have been written down any time between the twelfth and the fourteenth century, but by the end of the latter century two islands peculiarly linked with Ireland began to appear on those world maps which now gave additional space to the hitherto empty ocean lying westwards from Europe. The first, the Isle of Brasil, appears from early in the fourteenth century sometimes lying only a little to the west of Ireland but on

other charts farther to the west; and with it soon was
associated the Isle of St. Brendan usually placed a little farther
to the south.   Authors of sailing directions and chartmakers -
in the fifteenth century the ocean chart replaced or helped out
the older disc-like *mappemonde* - vied with each other to
place Brasil and St. Brendan's Isle in the ocean.   Indeed in
many cases they went so far as to indicate two of each.[1]

III.   Columbus, Brazil and Newfoundland

Columbus certainly visited Galway, most probably in 1477,
and saw on the Irish shore a dead man and woman who may
have been far lost Inuit (Eskimo).   But the long tradition that
an Irishman accompanied Columbus in 1492 was shattered
some years ago by Alice B. Gould who showed merely that
one Irishman had been on one American voyage before 1500 -
though at least this was an Irish contact with the New World
before its character and name had been established (since
Columbus believed down to the time of his death in 1506 that
he had found and been in Asia).
English contacts with the Newfoundland fishery may have
begun shortly after 1480 when the Bristol men began looking
for the Isle of Brasil and perhaps finding it in the form of
the fish-surrounded Newfoundland.   It has been suggested that
Irish links with early Atlantic exploration went further still.
The late F.R. Forbes Taylor considered he had established that
from 1479 onwards to at least 1503 the Bristol men who were
importing large quantities of fish, ostensibly from Ireland, were
in fact getting it from Newfoundland and arranging some
cover-up with their Irish contacts and perhaps associates in
Galway and elsewhere.   My own view is that Bristol ships
were getting the fish off Iceland, transhipping it at Galway,
and having it sent to Bristol as if it came from Ireland,

where it paid custom as it would not have done if it had come from Newfoundland. (This was because there was a royal embargo on Bristol trade with Iceland at the time, as a result of the monopoly claimed by the Hanseatic League.) But my view could be mistaken. We may not make too much of this yet it may not be entirely irrelevant to mention that Irish surnames like Teg and Flanagan turn up among the shippers of such cargoes in the Bristol customs accounts, even if most of the shippers were Englishmen from Bristol.

There is a possibility of an indirect contact between Ireland and Brazil at the very opening of the sixteenth century which has never been envisaged previously. Red dye in general, brought from the East Indies, was known as 'grain', but the red dye from a particular East Indian tree giving a particular shade of red was known as 'brasil'. Vasco da Gama probably brought some from India to Portugal in 1499, Cabral almost certainly did in 1501. But this same brazilwood (another species of the same *Caesalpinia)* was found in the New World. Pinzón brought 450 pounds of the wood to Spain and sold it in December 1500; he found it someplace along the northern coast of South America. Cabral discovered the east coast of Brazil in April 1500: he sent a ship back with news, and with some parrots, to Lisbon, but whether they brought brazilwood is not known. Vespucci refers to dyewoods from his voyage down the Brazilian coast in 1501 but again we do not know if he brought any back with him. It was not until 1503 that commercial exploitation of the brazilwood was begun by the Portuguese (and the name given to the land by Cabral, Santa Cruz, gradually gave way to Brazil).

On 6 October 1503 the ship *Frauncis* of Bristol brought into that port from Ireland 80 pounds of 'brasell' - the importer was William White but the Irish port of origin was not specified.[2] And then on 3 January 1504 the ship *Trinity* of Chepstow brought to Bristol from Ireland (the port again not specified) six and a half hundred weights of 'Brasell de terra nova', namely brazil from the New Lands, that is the Americas. It would seem therefore that a lading of brazilwood had reached an Irish port, most probably in August or September 1503 (the alternatives are Wexford or Waterford), from either Spain or Portugal as the result of a voyage to the New World. It might have been part of Pinzón's cargo sold in Spain in 1500. More probably it had been brought from Brazil, either by Vespucci or perhaps by a Portuguese expedition of which we do not know any details, in 1502 or 1503. In any case it must have reached Ireland by August or September 1503 at the earliest. Bristol customs officials knew about the New Land (*Terra Nova*) as the first known codfish from Newfoundland had been brought into that port in 1502, and no doubt Cabot's voyage of 1497 and those which followed were known also. It is, however, most extraordinary that the first known brazilwood from the New World should have reached Ireland before it came to England and that it was exported from Ireland to Bristol in October 1503 and January 1504.

In 1517 it was Waterford which had some indirect contact with the New World, this time North America. John Rastell, a brother-in-law of Sir Thomas More, decided in 1517 to search out a place for Englishmen to settle in North America, of which very little was known in England at the time. He sailed into Waterford Harbour in the *Barbara*, a London ship. But the crew struck. The purser of the *Barbara*, James Ravyn, incited the men against Rastell, and he had to abandon the voyage and send the ship back to England. The *Mary Barking*, her sister ship, had gone to Cork, had a similar mutiny and also returned to England. London seamen were evidently unwilling to entrust themselves to an ocean crossing to an unknown land. Rastell stayed on for a time in Waterford and lodged with a Waterford man, Thomas Dryvam or Bryver (the documents clearly were confused).[3] Rastell seems to have liked it there and so settled down to write *A new interlude and a mery of the iiij elements*, which he later published in London, the first English book with any detail about North America. He knew about the Newfoundland fishery and the extensive French participation in it. How much he informed his Waterford friends about America, and how much or how little they were able to tell him, we are wholly unable to say. It is not impossible, though there is no evidence for it, that Waterford may have begun to send a ship or two to Newfoundland even at this early date.

From 1502 onwards, when the first cargo of fish from there is known to have been brought to Europe, in this case to Bristol,[4] the Newfoundland fishery may already have begun to attract the Portuguese and they were soon followed by the French and a little later by the Spaniards. Well before the middle of the century it had become one of the greatest, if not the greatest, fishery in the western world. It had two separate branches - the first, the Banks fishery, where in shallow, misty water, cod were caught in great number on lines, and immediately salted down in the hold, and then brought as rapidly as possible to Europe. The other branch was the inshore fishery, where a ship found a secure harbour in the island and sent out boats to catch cod in inshore waters, after which the fish were prepared and set out to dry, with the addition of a little salt, on 'flakes' (platforms spread with green branches). This involved heavy labour, and consequently many ships carried extra men to do the hard work on shore of preparing the fish for its journey home, kept as dry as possible in the hold. We may wonder if, from early in its history, the inshore fishery did not have (as it was to have much later) many Irishmen among these labourers, who were picked up by ships on their outward voyage from England and brought back to their home ports when the ships returned in the autumn. But we have, for the early period, no evidence of this being done.

The major Irish ports could most probably have found and applied sufficient capital to engage in fishing off Newfoundland during the early sixteenth century, but the direct evidence that they did this is so far totally lacking. Such information as we have relates solely to Irish-based vessels which entered English ports with Newfoundland fish (designated as such) for sale. As these accounts are by no means complete, even they cannot indicate satisfactorily how extensive was the sale of Irish-caught Newfoundland fish in England. Ada Longfield, in her *Irish trade in the sixteenth century* (1929), recorded what she had found in the close examination she made of such sixteenth century customs records as survive, and a subsequent review of these sources has not added to what she recorded. The only additions have come through the examination of Chester local customs records, and something, more recently, from the miscellanea of the High Court of Admiralty.[5]

It may, however, be worth noting in detail what was carried in the earliest vessel recorded as having been to Newfoundland, namely the *Mighel* (*Michael*) of Kinsale, the record dated 6 November 1536. She had called at Kinsale on her return from her transatlantic voyage, in order to add some Irish products (such as wool) to her cargo. Her master, named John Colman, was evidently of Old English stock. The consignees of Newfoundland fish and oil, were respectively John Roche, also of Old English stock, and Edmond Molleye (Molloy?), who was probably Gaelic Irish, together with a foreigner, Martin Lubrin, origin unknown, but just possibly Flemish. The cargo of Newfoundland origin was as follows.

John Roche, denizen, 4½ M [5,400] salt fish of Terra Nova [Newfoundland] worth £30; 1 tun train oil [cod liver oil] worth £2. 6s. 8d. [and a few other goods], on which subsidy was paid of £1. 8s. 4d.

Edmond Molleye, denizen, 1 M [1,200] salt fish of Terra Nova, worth £6. 16s. 4d, and 1 tun of train oil worth £2. 6s. 8d [and some other goods], custom and subsidy 19s. $2^3/_4$d.

Martin Lubrin, alien, 1 M [1,200] salt fish of Terra Nova worth £6. 16s. 4d, 1 tun of train oil worth £2. 6s. 8d [and other goods], subsidy 16s. 5¼d.

These were sizeable amounts, if not large by the standards of English ships later in the century. We cannot judge them against strictly contemporary English imports as the latter were allowed in free of custom and subsidy, after a case in the Court of Exchequer in London in 1509, as a result of which they were not entered in the accounts.

Longfield records another Kinsale ship landing '400 fish of the small sort from Newfoundland'; and there was frequent Irish contact with Chester, which partly served as a supplier of fish to the English garrison in Ireland. In 1566 Robert Furlong of Wexford brought a mere 40 small Newfoundland fish to Chester (with other things), in the *Mary* of 'Heall' (an unidentified locality). By 1585 there was a much greater to-and-fro of fish between Ireland and Chester: thus, the *Sondaie* (*Sunday*) of Dublin brought 1½ M. [i.e. 1,800] Newfoundland fish to Chester. Furthermore, Sir Henry Wallop, writing to Sir Francis Walsingham on 19 August 1585, stated that he was sending him 'a sample of Ore from Newfoundland'. This indicates that Dublin ships were going to and from

Newfoundland and that someone had made an examination of minerals there, as Sir Humphrey Gilbert is known to have already done, in 1583. As early as 1580 an official order of fish for the Irish garrison detailed 20 M. (24,000) Newfoundland fish, and the order was apparently met, indicating that Chester was now a major entrepôt for the fish brought back, much of it, most likely, by Irish vessels.

The need to supply a growing military force in Ireland from this time on induced the Dublin merchant, Nicholas Weston, in 1596 to take a hand in the Newfoundland trade.[6] He was requested by the Dublin administration to send out two ships to provide fish and other necessities for the troops now deeply engaged in the Nine Years War. Weston could not, evidently, find seamen who would suit his purpose. He went to Poole for assistance and two Dublin ships were duly manned there and set to sea, Poole being a major port in the Newfoundland trade at this time, and probably one from which some of the Chester fish had come. In the event one ship was lost at sea, perhaps with all hands. Weston then bought a share in a Poole vessel which sailed to Newfoundland and returned with a reasonable catch. The Poole authorities stepped in, wishing to reserve the catch for sale locally. But official intervention from London and Dublin led to orders for the ship and her catch to be brought round to Dublin, William Pitt, the Poole merchant, and Thomas Newes, the master, being named as the persons responsible for the attempt to divert the lading. Probably the ship did reach Dublin: at least Weston late in the year brought a considerable quantity of fish - shore-dried cod, or 'Poor John' as the sailors called it - to Dublin for the army. Weston continued to supply the army with fish in the years following, but most probably obtained it from southern English ports, though it is possible he was himself sending out vessels to Newfoundland.

He was still involved in the trade in 1601, when he sent the *Lion* of Dublin to Spain with hides and a quantity of fish too rotten even for the soldiers to eat - and this in spite of the strict embargo which was laid at this time on any direct trade with Spain - he may have hoped to poison a few Spaniards in this way! In the same year he was under contract to supply the army, and once again used the *Lion* (60 tons), together with the *George* and the *Peter*, and with skeleton Irish crews, to go to Poole to collect experienced men, whom he hired himself, from Weymouth as well as Poole. The three vessels reached Newfoundland and fished between Baccalieu and Cape Race at the southeastern tip of Newfoundland, the *Lion* alone accumulating some 90,000 fish, it was claimed, worth £400-£500 in Dublin. However, she was unfortunate, running into the Spanish squadron guarding the Spanish invaders of Kinsale and was captured. She later escaped, but only to fall victim to an English privateer, her lading being disposed of at Falmouth. The other two vessels apparently also returned, but with what cargo is not known. This, however, was enough for Weston. Henceforth he bought his Newfoundland fish at Chester. Occasional ventures were apparently made by other ports, the ship of James Stafford of Wexford being seized by a pirate, Stephen Easton, at Newfoundland in 1612. As usual, however, it is only the ships which got into difficulties that appear in the surviving records. The truth probably is that several ports, notably Kinsale and Wexford, and perhaps Waterford, as well as Dublin, also engaged in the trade from time to time and that their ships brought their cargoes safely home. But it is impossible to estimate either the number of ships involved, or the significance of the Irish element in the overall growth of the fishery, which was attracting some 500 European ships a year in the early seventeenth century.

IV. *Irishmen and Spanish America*

If Irishmen in general had only the slightest contact with the New World in the sixteenth century, certain Irish individuals did have experience there through one means or another. Irishmen were adventurous and entered the Spanish service when they could, as soldiers of fortune. Some few of these served in Spanish America and it may be that a small number will be identifiable in the expeditions of Soto, Coronado, Luna and others.

From 1565 a few Irish would seem to have formed part of the garrison of Spanish Florida. A handful too were settlers in the attempted English colonies in Queen Elizabeth's Virginia (modern North Carolina). Irishmen were also sailors: few English ships sailed without one or two Irishmen in the crew and occasionally one of them stands out in some action or other. Irishmen served equally on the Spanish fleets. Hence at times during the long sea war from 1585 and 1604, Irishmen are likely to have met on opposite sides in engagements in American waters. Still other Irishmen went abroad as parish clergy or as Jesuit or Franciscan missionaries in the Spanish empire, Jesuits in particular to Brazil, and one or two came to serve their church in North America. Other Irish Catholics appear to have been associated, in the sixteenth century and early seventeenth century, with English Catholics in schemes to found American colonies where both Irish and English might follow their religious practices without interference. But before England and France began to establish permanent settlements in North America from 1607 on, it is possible to identify only a handful of Irishmen who spent time in North America.

We can, however, point out a few named individuals. San
Augustín in Florida was the first Spanish town in North
America. It had a parish priest from 1594 on (and the parish
register has survived): after a Spanish priest held the cure of
souls for a few months he was followed by Francis Marron,
an Irish priest of whom little is known. He in his turn was
succeeded in 1597 by Father Richard Arthur (Don Ricardo
Artur), a member of the well-known Limerick family and
evidently a personality of some importance in the little
community. He saw the impressive work of Franciscan
missionaries bear fruit in the rapid conversion of local Indians
and his greatest days were in 1606 when the Bishop of Cuba
came to confirm over 300 Spaniards and their earlier converts
and to baptise several thousand new Christians. A priest for
more than a decade, when few settlers stayed so long, Father
Arthur had a good deal to do with knitting this small frontier
post into a community.[7]

Irishmen like Fathers Marron and Arthur were aligned on
the Spanish side. Other Irishmen tended to shift between the
service of England and of Spain, sometimes betraying the
former to the latter. In the first English colonising expedition
in 1585 organised by Sir Walter Ralegh and led by Sir
Richard Grenville, at least four Irishmen remained in the
colony on Roanoke Island over the winter of 1585-6 - Edward
Nugent, Darby Glande or Glavin, Edward Kelly and John
Costigo (or Costigan). Nugent proved an effective aide to the
governor, Ralph Lane, chasing the Indian chief, Wingina, in
June 1586 and cutting his head off, when relations between
Indians and whites had deteriorated. Darby Glavin went back
to England with the rest, but had not enjoyed very much his
experiences as one of the first Irishmen to live in North
America for any length of time. He was persuaded in 1587,
perhaps because he could not obtain other employment, to join

a further expedition, which, under John White, was intended
to form the first real community settlement on Chesapeake
Bay. He had this time another Irish companion, Dennis
Carroll. The ships of this expedition called in for rest and
water at Puerto Rico, and there the two Irishmen deserted and
were eventually picked up by the Spaniards. We hear nothing
more about Carroll: as for Glavin, he was not taken at his
own value as an Irishman who had, against his will, been
impressed on two English voyages to an area the Spaniards
regarded as their own. He was therefore tried and was duly
sentenced to the galleys. He must have maintained there his
claim to be a good Catholic since he was eventually released,
on condition he became a soldier. About 1595 he was
brought from Cuba to San Augustín in Florida and under the
name of David Glavin, was duly installed as a member of the
garrison there. In 1600 he had an opportunity to tell the
governor, Méndez de Canzo, about his earlier experiences on
Roanoke Island. His tale was a rather tall one. The
colonists grew wheat and barley (which in fact they were
unable to do). There was a lot of gold and he gave some
details of its fineness (but there was none). There were many
pearls: one as big as an acorn was taken from him by Sir
Richard Grenville. This is less unlikely although the size is
improbable. He thought the colony from which he deserted
in 1587 was still in existence on Chespeake Bay, where the
governor pressed him to go and spy it out.[8] From that point
he fades back into oblivion and probably died in Florida -
where he may have had Father Arthur to comfort him.

John Martin, alias William Cornelius, a sweeper (the lowest
form of nautical life) on John Hawkins' 1567-8 flagship, the
Jesus of Lubeck, which was put out of action at San Juan de
Ulua in 1568, was not so fortunate. He was one of her
crew who reached the *Minion* and escaped in her, but he

happened to be one of the 100 men landed by the over-laden Hawkins on the northern shore of Mexico and eventually he was captured by the Spaniards. The episcopal inquisition in Mexico City was replaced in 1570 by the Holy Office, the rigid state instrument which had rooted out heresy in Spain. One result in Mexico was that many of the English captives, who had originally been given light sentences or none, were re-examined. All but one of the first forty tried before the new body were given penalties short of death when they claimed that they had abjured Protestantism and become Catholics. It was not until 1574 that John Martin (Juan Martinez) was rounded up at La Trinidad, where he had married and carried on the craft of a barber, and taken before the Inquisition. He declared that he had been brought up in Cork but it became clear that he and his mother had gone to England when he was quite young and that at Padstow he had conformed to the Church of England, before he went to sea. He claimed to have maintained at all times that he was Irish and as such was subjected to abuse on board ship. During a long examination, punctuated by torture, he gave conflicting accounts of his beliefs and allegiances, but stubbornly insisted he had remained a Catholic at heart throughout his period with the English. Had he confessed to having been a Protestant and maintained that he abjured his heresy he would have escaped the ultimate penalty, but his insistence that as a Catholic he had taken part in heretical practices put him outside the pale of the inquisitors' thinking. He was eventually condemned to be 'relaxed', and was handed over to the secular arm to be garrotted and his body burned, at the auto-da-fé in Mexico City on 6 March 1575. Professor Hair's penetrating account of his career between 1568 and 1574 and of his trial and condemnation, is a fine piece of historical reconstruction.[9] It illustrates, however, the risks which an

Irish Catholic could run, through his own ignorance of the correct plea to obtain eventual forgiveness from an over-subtle Holy Office.

There were other Irishmen in Mexico. It appears from the records of John Martin's trial that Diego Suarez, another barber who had lived long in Mexico, was Irish too, though his Irish name is unknown. Another Irishman, possibly from the same group as John Martin, John Brown (Juan Brun), was reconciled to the Catholic church after trial. Further investigation may well reveal that Mexico and other Spanish-American territories sheltered and gave opportunities to other Irishmen whose beliefs and practices raised no religious problem.

A more fortunate Irishman than the hapless John Martin was also involved in these English voyages to North America. Richard Butler was born in Waterford but went to England when young and entered the service of Sir Walter Ralegh. He was sent by Ralegh on the reconnaissance voyage in 1584 which discovered Roanoke Island and prepared the way for the colony. In 1585 he went out once more with Sir Richard Grenville to the newly-named Virginia, but did not remain, as the Irish party already mentioned did, with the governor, Ralph Lane, over the winter, but came back to England. Thus blooded, he went on to serve on a privateer owned by Ralegh and eventually rose to be a privateering captain during the hectic years between 1587 and 1590, when he clearly did much damage to Spain. In 1593, however, he sailed on another privateer belonging to the earl of Cumberland, and, with a friend of Irish parentage, named Roche, had himself landed on the Portuguese coast. From there he got in touch with several persons who were suspected of being agents for the English, with the result that he and his friend were apprehended as spies. He now claimed that he had

deliberately escaped from the English because he was a
Catholic and an Irishman. At least his religion passed muster,
as he was visited in gaol by the Irish Jesuit, James Archer,
but he was treated nonetheless as if indeed an English spy.
The historian, Richard Stanyhurst (of whom there has been a
recent biography), by then in Spain, was called in to interpret
at several interrogations. Butler told much about his two
voyages to America - and a good deal that is of value - and
he talked freely of his life and contacts in England. But his
requests to be allowed to serve Spain were refused and he
was eventually tried and sentenced to death for espionage, a
sentence that was commuted to life service in the galleys.
Few men survived that kind of slavery for more than a few
years (if so long) but Butler was apparently tough as well as
lucky. Fifteen years later, in 1608, he emerged and returned
to England, during a brief period of relaxation in Anglo-
Spanish relations.[10] By then his American experiences had
most likely faded from his memory. Whether he returned to
Waterford to die we do not know.

V. Irish Settlers in Virginia

These little scraps of personal histories tell us something
about Irishmen in America, but little or nothing about
Ireland's relationship with that western continent. Indeed,
before 1600, apart from the fishery, contacts were indirect.
Englishmen planned colonies in Ireland and tried unsuccessfully
to set them up; then the same Englishmen - Sir Humphrey
Gilbert, Sir Walter Ralegh, Ralph Lane and Sir Richard
Grenville among them - busied themselves in the 1580s trying
to establish colonies in North America at the same time as
they or their agents were trying to build up properties in
Munster. When the American ventures broke down and John

White, governor of Ralegh's last colony, lost contact with the colonists he conveyed to America in 1587 - the Lost Colonists of North American myth - he came to Munster to settle and may have died there. For a time too, the great scientist, Thomas Harriot, who had been with White in the 1585-6 colony on Roanoke Island, came to live on the Blackwater at Molana Abbey, on lands in the possession of Sir Walter Ralegh, and there were others ex-colonists who did the same.[11] Ireland was an alternative colony to America for certain Englishmen. But the writer Richard Hakluyt argued instead that if the English settled in North America it would create a great trade with Ireland and would thus help to pacify that country. He was only partly right.[12]

Then, too, many Englishmen spoke of the Gaelic Irish and the Amerindian inhabitants of North America in similar terms. Both were wild and savage, cunning and treacherous, scarcely civil in their habits, dress, even beliefs. This meant, perhaps, that they considered the Irish and the Indians to be beyond some English pale, and therefore people who could be treated as less than human. Englishmen, like most Europeans, were xenophobic in their nationalism at this time. But they did not necessarily regard all Irishmen as inferior, or all Indians either, though they could and did treat them on occasion as if they deserved little consideration as human beings. But then they would probably have treated in a similar way any people who did not speak English and/or live exactly as the English did, the Welsh and Scots, for example, in times of rebellion or war.

It was really only when the sixteenth was turning into the seventeenth century that Ireland began seriously to be involved in the Americas. As the Nine Years War was coming to an end the question of what to do with all the Irish soldiers who were going to be out of employment (and probably prove unemployable by the English) became serious. From 1600 onwards there was a regular suggestion - send them to America. Many of the Irish fled to France or Spain or Portugal after the Counter-Reformation failure at Kinsale in 1601. In France the authorities considered shipping some Irish to Canada in 1605 though they did not do so.[13]   The Spaniards (and the Jesuits) vetoed a proposal that soldiers discharged from the Spanish forces after the Treaty of London in 1604, many of them Irish, should be settled under English Catholic gentlemen in Maine in North America.[14]   Only the Portuguese acted. In 1605 they sent an Irish contingent to Brazil, where many are thought to have died in wars with the local Indians.[15]   In 1607 an English soldier, Richard Bingley, tried to assemble ships, first in Dublin Bay and then at Kinsale, ostensibly to establish an English colony in America, but this was only a cover for piracy against Spain, now at peace with England, and was soon exposed as a deception. Bingley was protected by Lord Deputy Chichester, founder of modern Belfast.[16]

Even after Englishmen had begun to establish a permanent colony in Virginia there were fresh plans in 1609 to send Irishmen en masse to defend the English colony there against a possible Spanish attack, following a less clearly defined project to do the same in 1607.[17]   But all the English plans for systematic use of Irish soldiers in North America came to nothing. There was clearly little enthusiasm on the part of the Irish to go, and the English had, on each occasion, second thoughts about the wisdom of sending Irishmen to live in English outposts in North America, when they could not be trusted to remain obedient to their leaders or, indeed, not to hand over their settlement to the Spaniards.

Before exploring the new circumstances of the seventeenth century, let me give just one more example of an Irishman who visited America. In May 1607 Christopher Newport safely conveyed the members of the expedition that was to found the first permanent English settlement in North America up the great river which they christened the James, to the site for their settlement they chose to call Jamestown. The Irishman, Francis Magnel, was one of the party of pioneers who stayed for a year to establish this bridgehead. He survived, as few did, the first hard winter, and so was allowed to come back to England on one of the supply vessels which relieved the colony at the beginning of 1608. Although it was thought at the time that he might be a Spanish spy, it was not until 1610 that he was persuaded to go to Spain and tell the Spaniards something about the English colony.[18] His description of Virginia was only a moderately useful one since the English did not achieve much in 1607-8 on account of epidemics. Magnel's report contained a few of the kind of exaggerations we have noted in the earlier tale of Darby Glavin. Magnel understood, for example, that the local Indians had told the English that the South Sea (the Pacific) was only a short distance away and that the western American shores were peopled by a race who wore red silk robes and were rich in gold. He exaggerated the whole scale of the enterprise, saying the English intended to put 20,000 to 30,000 men into Virginia, and would do so in order to harm the king of Spain. He was not taken too seriously and was not offered a place in the Spanish service as he had hoped, though a Spanish reconnaissance vessel attempted in 1611 to follow up the information he had supplied, with only very limited success. But Magnel is something of a hangover from the tentative small-scale connections of the sixteenth century.

What really made the difference in the first forty years of the seventeenth century? In the first place, and principally, planting colonies became big business for Englishmen. The replanting of Munster, the colonising of Virginia, attempted plantations and colonies in Guiana, on the Amazon, and in the Leeward Islands, the unsuccessful colony in Maine in 1607, the Ulster plantation, the colonising of Newfoundland, the plantation of Wexford, Longford and the rest, all flowed on during the later part of the reign of James I. One thing that this meant was that a class of land speculators grew up. They might get a footing in one part of Ireland, then take up another quite different venture in Virginia, and finally come back to a further plantation in Ireland. There were only a few who did this but they were the heralds of the new land-speculating imperialism of the time.

Then too, plantations needed men. Virginia at the start needed men from whatever source she could get them. Most men went to Virginia under contract. Some had crafts and specialised skills to sell and could sell them. But most had no money and only their labouring bodies to dispose of; hence they contracted with speculators who carried them overseas and recouped themselves by selling their labour services for a term of years - the indentured labourer having the chance of some free land and/or some money and/or equipment only if he stayed out his term, under a master, for from three to seven years. Four types of person were available in Ireland. First, Englishmen who were lesser tenants and labourers and had come over to Irish plantations but who were dissatisfied there or were tempted by potential high rewards overseas. Second, the sturdy, labouring Irish, men and women, who wanted employment where their robust but simple skills could win them means of subsistence and perhaps a little more - though in fact not very many indentured labourers of this type survived to claim their free portions of land when they had served their time. Virginia, where Jamestown was founded in 1607 and which went through various vicissitudes between then and 1617, suddenly became attractive to speculators. On the one hand the Virginia Company expanded its own commitment and raised the possibility of many more indentured labourers being needed; on the other it offered 'particular plantations' free of its control to speculators. Some of the latter were found in Munster. A third group of Irish emigrants, a very small one, was composed of major undertakers in Munster who wished to experiment in profitable exploitation of land on the other side of the Atlantic as well as in Ireland. Finally, a fourth group consisted of some of the Old English landowners deprived of land by confiscation.

Three Munster adventurers came to play an active part in Virginia. Captain William Nuce, an English soldier, made a business of going round Munster after the war was over in 1603 and acquiring, by one means or another, lands in various seignories on which he placed tenants on long leases, from these deriving an income even when the seignories were formally allotted to other undertakers.[19] He had a hand in setting up the Bandon seignory, of which the earl of Cork was to make such a signal success, and then moved up the Bandon River to establish his own seignory of Newcetown, which seems to have been moderately successful, having twenty-four houses in 1622 with, perhaps, a hundred settlers. Well before that time he had placed this plantation under other management. In April 1620 he proposed to the Virginia Company of London that, in return for bringing a thousand people (largely we might assume from Ireland), he should be granted a particular plantation (as a private estate) in Virginia and that he should be appointed marshal, that is, head of the armed forces in the colony. These ambitious propositions were accepted in May 1621, and between then and 21 April 1621 he made an expedition to Virginia to obtain his grant of land in the Kecoughtan Peninsula; and also, to pay for the grant, made a flying visit to Ireland, where he put Newcetown under a manager. He took back with him to America in October 1621, it would appear, further colonists, again it is probable from Ireland, though the original labourers on his land, indentured servants, were said to be in poor shape, perhaps from disease. His military duties, as reported to the Company from Virginia were well done, that is, he had performed well during the Indian rising of March 1622. But he may have been wounded since he was reported as having died in April 1622. This report was not confirmed in time to stop a knighthood being conferred on him by James I in June, thus posthumously.

His brother, Captain Thomas Nuce, had also certainly served with him in Munster, though he has not been identified so far among the settlers. He put himself forward to the Virginia Company in May 1620 for the post of 'deputy', that is, collector of the Company's rents from its tenants, and he also asked for a 'particular plantation'. He was duly appointed as 'deputy' for the southern part of the colony and his private plantation was laid out at the tip of the Kecoughtan Peninsula, where he developed part of Elizabeth City, soon an important settlement, though we do not know that he brought settlers from Ireland to it. In the Indian rising of 24 March 1622 he put up a stout defence, trying to pull the colonists together after the rising, forcing them to plant crops, and himself building houses, in close co-operation with Daniel Gookin, at Newport News. He exerted himself so much that he fell ill and died early in 1624. The Nuce (or Newce) brothers were thus prominent for a short time in Virginia, but left little mark either there or in Munster, though both Newcetown and Elizabeth City continued to survive, and the latter to grow.

Daniel Gookin was the other Munster planter who was to be closely associated with Virginia.[20] He obtained and settled the seignory of Carrigaline, south of Cork and near Cobh, where he apparently concentrated on raising cattle, goats and other stock imported from England. On 13 November 1620 he offered to transport cattle and provisions to Virginia, but agreement by the Company was slow to come. Only in July 1621 was it agreed he should do so. He asked for £11 for each heifer of English stock and for each she-goat: he settled for £10 in the end but found, when he went to Virginia, that he was paid only in tobacco, one hundredweight for each cow. He asked for and obtained a grant of a 'particular plantation', on terms not less favourable than William Newce had obtained, and got what he wanted at Newport News, close to Elizabeth City, 150 acres initially and more later. He soon returned to Munster and prepared an expedition. His ship, the *Flying Hart*, made a rapid voyage with 50 adventurers, some as tenants, others as labourers, who bound themselves to work for him for a term of years in return for a guarantee of free land at the end of the term. He also carried 30 passengers for other planters. The ship arrived on 22 November 1621. His cattle and goats were highly regarded and he was able to establish a strong post at Newport News and sail back to Ireland or England with his tobacco. A man of great energy, he was soon to collect a further cargo of settlers and provisions. It is ironical that the Council in Virginia, recording his first arrival, wrote to the parent body in London, 'we do conceave great hope (yf the Irish Plantacione prosper) that frome Ireland great multitudes of People will be like to come hether.' Indeed, while Gookin was still waiting in 1621 to have his proposals approved by the Virginia Company, a number of potential competitors from Ireland appeared, offering to bring cattle to Virginia in great quantities at lower rates than Gookin was demanding, but none are known to have succeeded in doing this.

In the spring of 1622 Gookin's men were hard at work clearing ground for the plantation of tobacco. The Indian rising of 22 March 1622 caught many in the fields and all but seven of these indentured servants were killed, according to the only report we have. How many dead in all there were is not known (indeed the detailed report of the rising denies that any were killed in this area, even though Thomas Nuce had to fight off attackers at nearby Elizabeth City and aided in the defence of Newport News).[21] Some 35 persons were inside the settlement after the rising: a new arrival wrote on 24 April that 'he found at his landing out of the *Abigaile* the Governor [Sir George Yardley] and his lady at Master Gookings Plantacion'. But 'his Plantacion [was] ready to fall into decay'. Nevertheless, after a long and difficult voyage Gookin arrived back at his depleted estate in the *Guidance* of Bristol, jointly owned by Gookin and John Ewing, with 40 more labourers and 30 passengers, though the passengers were in poor shape. He put in early in April, but with few provisions remaining to help relieve the stricken colony, though at least 40 cattle had survived. About this time, too, other speculators offered the Company to transport out of Ireland '20 or 30 able youths of 16 or 17 years of age to Virginia to be apprenticed for 6 or 7 years', and the arrangement was agreed in principle. But this was before news of the rising reached England and the promoters may then have retired from the fray, since nothing more than an acceptance in principle of their offer has been found. Gookin seems thenceforth to have divided his time between Ireland and Virginia and to have limited his operations, since in January 1625 there were only 25 men (and no women) at his plantation and in his house, Maries Mount.

Daniel Gookin retained his dual concern with Ireland and Virginia until his death in 1633. He appears to have resided most of the time in Munster, where he retained his base in the Carrigaline plantation (until it passed into Robert Boyle's hand), though he may have continued sending cattle and provisions to Virginia. He left his Newport News plantation at first to managers, though from 1631 to 1643 it was run by his sons, who eventually sold it in the latter year, after continued ownership by a Munster planter family for twenty-two years. Gookin was very much a projector as well as a planter. He was involved in a company to plant Guiana and the Amazon in 1627, and in 1631 showed his credulity by proposing to occupy the 'Isle of Brasil', the mythical island which from the fifteenth century onwards had appeared on so many charts of the Atlantic, and was actually given a patent to do so![22]

The fieldworkers who were killed in 1622 were almost certainly native Irish, though those who set up the little town of Newport News need not have been. Indeed, MacCarthy-Morrogh is probably right when he says that the 25 people at Newport News in 1625 bore no Irish or Old English names (though John Barratt and William Croney might be exceptions). It is clear, however, that the promoters who were in the field in 1622 offering to bring out youths under indenture were proposing to bring native Irish, and that it was these who were expected to do the heavy labour in the colony. The English hangers-on, who may have come from Munster, were instead looking for land, or else for occupations in the settlements that were springing up, where there were chances of either acquiring free tenancies to smaller portions of land or fulfilling the role of craftsmen. Much still remains to be clarified but it is clear that the Nuce brothers and Daniel Gookin were genuine pioneers in the beginning of both the emigration process from Ireland and the provision trade to America, and as such are worth remembering.

Under Company rule before 1624 there appears to have been no rigid proscription of Irish Catholics from settling in Virginia. In 1620, indeed, we have a list of Wexford landlords (both Old English and Gaelic Irish), who had been expelled from their lands and had failed to get redress of their grievances from the Irish Privy Council, but whom the English Privy Council undertook to get out of the way by 'restrayning some of them to send to Virginia'.[23]   Whether they actually went and if so whether they were assimilated there or turned away is not clear. Similarly, the lord deputy in 1630 ordered a number of dispossessed Old English landlords in Waterford to be sent to Virginia, but in this case we know that they were turned away by the colonists, the ruling élite having decided that only conforming Anglicans should settle there.[24] After 1630 there is no indication that Virginia, indeed, was offered any Irish emigrants, even though English indentured servants continued to go there in increasing numbers. The Black servants who were gradually enslaved were not expected to turn Anglican, but Irishmen who were likely to be persistent Catholics were wholly unwelcome.

In the 1630s there was a continuing strong demand from Virginia for men, but also a new and growing demand from the Caribbean islands under English rule. Thomas Anthony was one entrepreneur willing to act as an agent to recruit in Ireland.[25]   In April 1636 he arranged for the ship *Abraham*, owned by Matthew Cradock, to go to Kinsale in the expectation of getting a cargo of Irish men and women for disposal in Virginia, or at least so he said. When he arrived at Kinsale, well ahead of the ship, he found he had to compete with a Dutch ship whose captain was already signing on labourers for the West Indies. He clearly had already many contacts in Munster (this venture was not his first) and so he set out to publicize his project, though he would not sign on anyone until the ship arrived, as he would have to spend too much on their keep in the meantime. He busied himself in preparing clothing for the emigrants by giving employment to local tailors, craftsmen and merchants - woollen and linen cloth, buttons, and so on are in his list of payments. When the ship came in August he hired agents to attend the markets in Cork, Bandon and Youghal, beating their drums and making their spiel about the advantages of life in Virginia, and inviting those who wished to emigrate to come to Kinsale to make their contracts. Some other of his agents appear to have signed on servants by trickery and one was punished at Kinsale for this. By mid-October Anthony had procured 41 men and 20 women, many of them seemingly native Irish, if not as many as he had hoped for. The women were described as from '17 to 35 years and very lusty and strong bodies which will I hope, said [Anthony], be means to set them off to the best advantage'. The women were more keen to go than the men. Setting out for England in November, Anthony found that his London backers had decided the party would not go to Virginia after all but to Barbados, where sale prospects were better.

The ship's passage to the Caribbean must have been a good one. Of the 56 who actually sailed (five having drifted off - mostly women because they were pregnant), 53 arrived, a high proportion, so that accommodation on board must have been fairly reasonable. They were duly 'disposed of to sale' for 27,650 pounds of tobacco, just as they would have been in Virginia. Anthony was clearly a conscientious man who did his best for his cargo, but the object of the exercise was to profit by the disposal of Irish muscle. How they fared in the end is not known. Anthony's letters indicate that he continued to operate vigorously in the following years down to 1641, during which he openly indicated he was recruiting for the West Indies, and found his would-be clients persistent in their requests for information on their prospects as servants and subsequently after they gained their freedom.

VI. Irish Settlers in Newfoundland

The case of Newfoundland in relation to Ireland in the early seventeenth century is rather different. It was a period when English participation in the inshore fishery was growing by leaps and bounds. By 1620 one estimate puts the numbers of English ships at 250 and the seamen they carried at 5,000. The ships also carried some 350 labourers (later known as 'green men'), who were employed on shore jobs during the summer so that the catch could be duly processed before the ships sailed. It is probable that there were an appreciable number of Irishmen amongst the seamen and a large number amongst the labourers. Moreover, from 1611 on, English colonies were being established in Newfoundland, which it was thought were capable of becoming self-sufficient and able to raise profitable returns from furs, fish and oil, even though the frequently hard winters deterred many who considered settling there.

In the second stage of settlement Irish Catholics played a significant part.[26] Between 1616 and 1621 four divisions of land in the Avalon Peninsula were granted to speculators by the original Newfoundland Company of 1610. Three were of some significance for Ireland. One grant of land was to William Vaughan and the land was occupied for some years by Welshmen who eventually went home. Vaughan sold off part of his grant to Henry Cary, including his original settlement site at Renews. Meanwhile Sir George Calvert had obtained a considerable slice of land south of St. John's. From 1621 his agent, Edward Wynne, was managing a colony for him at Ferryland, and a second agent joined him in 1622, to assist in the building of a substantial manor house. These first colonists, though probably mainly Catholics, are not known to have been Irish; and with them the colony made headway. But Calvert also obtained land in Ireland, in County Longford in 1619 and a little later in Wexford, where he built himself a house at Cloghhammon. In 1622 Henry Cary sent out Sir Francis Tanfield with colonists to Renews, and in the same year Cary was created Viscount Falkland and made lord deputy of Ireland. He knew Calvert, and in 1623, the two joined forces to plan a major colonial settlement using settlers of both sexes who would be assembled in Ireland. Their plan was primarily to get settlers for Falkland's lands, but Calvert had some say in the project.

The result was the publication in Dublin of the first colonising promotion pamphlet to appear there. *A short discourse of the New-found-land* (1623) is a very rare publication. It was credited to a certain T.C., who may have been Thomas Cary, an associate of both Falkland and Calvert. Falkland had been in touch with Richard Whitbourne, who had been in Newfoundland several times and had published tracts about it in London in 1620 and 1622, so that some of the 'inducements' in the Dublin tract may well have been derived from him. It was claimed that a colony would 'propagate' religion and open the way to converting the savage natives to Christianity. Officially then, its appeal was to Protestants, namely recent settlers dissatisfied with their situation in Ireland, as we have seen a few of those in Munster had become and so gone to Virginia. But it must have been primarily aimed, in Ireland, at those Catholic landowners who had been deprived of their lands in Longford, King's County,

Wexford and elsewhere in recent years, or who were in fear
of further disruption even if they had not yet been touched.
These were people who might be attracted to Calvert, a
crypto-Catholic (until 1625), and might have preferred their
chances at Ferryland to those in Renews. Ireland, it was
said, would benefit from such a colony by supplying
provisions and livestock (as we have seen had happened in
relation to Virginia) and it would also encourage the
development of shipbuilding and the supply of ships' stores in
a still economically under-developed country. The fishery was
a major attraction, not to be despised by gentlemen, as
fortunes were being made in the summer fishery - a correct
statement. One thing which could be profitably manufactured
in Newfoundland was salt, which otherwise had to be brought
expensively from Europe (in practice a most unlikely
alternative).

The climate, according to Falkland's agent, Wynne, who in
1622 had sent home a pamphlet to be published, was no
worse than that of England in winter and hotter in summer,
though icebergs kept the shore waters cool until well into
summer. There were trees available for any purpose, from
masts to firewood (but the trees were all conifers), and there
were plenty of birds, including 'Partridges [and] Pheasants'
(which was scarcely accurate though ptarmigan would qualify
in a loose sort of way), and freshwater as well as sea fish.
English vegetables would grow there well - this had been
established by the first colonists of 1611, at least as far as
carrots and turnips were concerned. Wheat and vines would
grow there too (a claim of some considerable doubt). Of
domestic animals, pigs and goats especially were known to
flourish. Investment was very cheap: £10 would secure a
small holding; £100 an estate of 2,000 acres. It would be
possible to recruit labourers in Newfoundland since the fishing

vessels (as has been noted) carried a number of men surplus to their crew to undertake summer work connected with the inshore fishery. These men could, it was thought, be recruited by the settlers. Passage from Britain and Ireland to Newfoundland was rapid and fishing vessels returning in the autumn gave a means of maintaining regular communications. An agent to collect subscribers was named for London as well as for Dublin, but it was hoped most settlers would go from 'this Kingdom [Ireland], where the name of a Plantation is so farre from being a stranger, as it hath beene the originall cause [from] which very many have derived their happinesse' (even if from it very many more had derived their unhappiness!). In the event, Falkland appears to have obtained few Protestant colonists (we do not know, however, how insistent he was on this or even how far he insisted that the project should exclude Catholics), as can be inferred from the fact that the colony expanded very little and that Tanfield returned home in 1626. The colony faded out shortly afterwards, in spite of projects in 1628 to revive it.

But this project was an essential preliminary exercise for Calvert. Relinquishing his post as secretary of state to Charles I when he avowed his Catholic allegiance in 1625, he was created Lord Baltimore of Baltimore, County Longford. He was then awarded a charter granting him the whole Avalon peninsula, though he was presumably expected to respect the existing rights of other promoters. He quickly replaced Wynn with a Catholic English gentleman, Sir Arthur Aston, but his own departure from England was delayed. Aston brought out fifteen Irish Catholics early in 1627, and with them two priests, Fathers Smith and Longeville, the first Catholic clergy to be sent to an English colony in the west, though it is uncertain how long they stayed. The Catholics were probably Old English Catholics dispossessed in Ireland, or threatened with dispossession. Baltimore paid a short visit to Newfoundland in 1627 and evidently was so impressed by what had been done since 1621 that he decided in 1628 to move to Ferryland, himself, his family, and his servants. This time there were forty colonists, the majority, we presume, being from Ireland. The Ferryland colony had had some Protestants in it too, including the Rev. Erasmus Stourton, an Anglican clergyman, who soon quarrelled with Baltimore and accused him and his priest, Father Hacket, of importing papacy to Newfoundland, and even of forcibly converting Protestants. Though Baltimore settled in comfortably for the summer and autumn, the winter proved a shock. Hemmed in by snow and ice, and probably finding the housing too flimsy to repel the chill, by spring 1629 he was considering leaving, and in August, before he actually left, he wrote a bitter attack on Newfoundland as a home for Europeans. With his family and many of his settlers, he sailed to Virginia, where the Anglican governor refused him permission to settle, so that he eventually arrived home in England, more or less disillusioned. His colonists hung on at Ferryland: there were fish to be caught and French prizes (for a time) to be taken, but gradually in the early 1630s the Ferryland colony faded until it was taken over by David Kirke in 1637. Up to that date it had had a Calvert-appointed governor and presumably enjoyed some measure of viability.

Ireland had thus gained in Newfoundland another foothold in North America. The colonists who remained there after 1637 may well have included a few Irish; it is even more likely that Irish labourers continued to come with the inshore fishing fleets and went home in the autumn. But we need much more evidence before any coherent story of the activities of these Irish can be attempted.

In Virginia, Newfoundland and Maryland in North America, and also in the Amazon and some West Indian islands, Irishmen could venture fairly freely, either as adventurers, paying their own way and bringing out others, or as indentured labourers. In Virginia they might have to give some nominal degree of recognition to the established Church of England, particularly when, over time, the Virginia establishment became rigidly Anglican. Yet with the scattered plantation type of settlement Catholics neither could nor would be normally obliged to go to church, albeit they would lack the services of their priests. In Maryland, however, and at least at times in Newfoundland, they would be in communities where they had not only co-religionists as countrymen, but also clergy to minister to them.[27] There seems to have been, though we still know little about its precise extent, a slow trickle of Catholic Irishmen to all these areas. But, remembering Daniel Gookin and his settlers at Newport News, we must not forget that New English from the planted areas, as well as Old English and Gaelic Irish, could find attractions in these colonies. Indeed it is probable that New English formed the majority of investors, though not necessarily of the settlers, in the 1623 colony in Newfoundland (but as investors they are not likely to have been very numerous).

VII. Would-be Settlers in New England

As far as Irishmen were concerned, the position of New England was very different. The Pilgrims of 1620 who founded Plymouth colony were radical Protestants and proved most unwilling to allow any practising Anglicans, let alone Catholics, into their tiny community, which in twenty years only grew from about 100 settlers to about 600. Massachusetts, when it was founded in 1630 with 1,000 people at one landing, was on a different scale. Whole families, many with relatives and servants, came out, transporting, in a sense, communities in east and southeast England to America. They did not formally break with the Church of England, but the reformed church they created in their new Commonwealth made a fairly clear breach with the episcopal system. In Massachusetts orthodox Anglican services were not allowed, but visiting or settling Anglicans could attend their own churches without difficulty, so long as they did not try to use the Book of Common Prayer, or advocate the introduction of bishops. Catholics on the other hand were anathema. If a Catholic came to the colony and failed to conform, at least to some extent, he would find there was no place for him: he soon left, even if he was not always officially forced to go. (It is possible that a handful went on to New Hampshire or Maine.) Hence there was no opening in New England for any of the Irish or Old English who wished either to sell their labour or to recoup their fortunes by acquiring new estates in America in place of those they had lost to the planters at home.

John Winthrop the younger, whose father was governor and became the patriarch of the Commonwealth, came over from America for a year in 1632-33 to study at Trinity College, Dublin (which professed a more puritan form of anglicanism than would be found in Oxford or Cambridge at this time). While in Ireland he made many contacts with the planter class, in both Dublin and the Pale and in Ulster. Shortly after he returned to Massachusetts, a friend, Edward Howes, wrote to him. It is a revealing letter:[28]

> You shall also recieve in this shipp 3 woolfe doggs and a bitch with an Irish boy to tend them. For the doggs my master hath writt sufficiently, but for the boye thus much. You have been in Ireland, knowe partlie the Irish condition.

This is a very tractable fellowe and yet of a hardie and stout corage. I am persuaded he is very honest, especially he makes great conscience of his promise and vowe.... At his first comminge over [to England] he would not goe to church nor come to prayers.... I hope with Gods grace he will become a good convert. *Converte graditim.* Sir, I dare boldlie saye it is as much honor for you to win this fellowes soule ... as to winn an Indians soule out of the Divells clawes.

In other words, the wolfhounds needed some expert Irish care to allow them to be used in hunting, but the young man sent with them might prove less malleable material. He was a Catholic; he had conformed on the surface in England, but would he accept the more demanding Puritan claims on him when he reached New England? I have not discovered how the 'Irish boy' got on in New England, but equally I cannot find any evidence that Winthrop asked for more of his like - Irish Catholics - to follow him. Among the over 22,000 persons who have been traced as migrating to New England before the end of 1649, only eleven appear to have been Irish.

If the connections between Ireland and New England were tenuous this was partly because of one project for emigration that failed. This involved the Scottish planters in Ulster.[29] They had moved in great numbers across the narrow channel between southern Scotland and northern Ireland to settle easily into the planted lands, not only of the six escheated counties but also of much of Antrim and Down, and had there created holdings which gave them a fair living. But to them too, as to the Catholics, their religion was vital. They had tried conscientiously to fit their Scottish ecclesiastical system, with its rather powerless bishops existing within a Presbyterian context, to Irish conditions, and at the start had had some

success.   But the rise of opposition in Scotland to Stuart
religious policy gradually made them uneasy in Ireland, while
a strong wave of evangelical fervour made them resistant to
even the somewhat Puritan framework of the established church
in Ireland.   Once the old Scottish king, James I, was gone,
new bishops in Ireland, and from 1633 onwards Thomas
Wentworth, now chief governor, turned the Scottish settlers (or
a substantial part of them) into enemies of the regime
administered from Dublin.   Their ministers could see that the
network of state power was being developed to strangle their
activities in Ulster.   They were strongly reinforced when
leaders of the Presbyterian resistance to the anglicizing church
policies of Charles I in the Scottish church took refuge with
them in Ireland.   And so the radicals amongst the planters
began to look for a place of refuge still further away from
Scotland than Ulster, where they, like those other Puritans
who were building Massachusetts, might be really free.

In February 1634 some of the Scottish planters felt they
had had enough.   Economically they had done well but they
had not the freedom in church matters they desired.   In
February 1634 it was decided that the Reverend John
Livingston, representing the ministers, and William Wallace,
representing the gentlemen, should take passage to
Massachusetts to agree with the governor and council for a
place to settle in.   They dallied on their way to London and
the ships they aimed for had already sailed for Boston.
Along with one of the Massachusetts men, John Humphrey,
they rode to Weymouth and picked up the fleet there, but
Wallace fell ill and was put ashore, with Livingston to look
after him, at Plymouth.   Humphrey duly delivered letters from
the two Ulster delegates to the governor and John Winthrop
noted in his diary in July: 'We received letters from a godly
preacher, Mr. Levinston, a Scotchman in the north of Ireland,

whereby he signified, that there were many good Christians in those parts resolved to come hither, if they might receive satisfaction concerning some questions and propositions which they sent over'. His answering letters, which have not survived, evidently gave satisfactory replies to the Ulstermen, since preparations were at once put in hand by the more determined Presbyterians to sacrifice their Irish fortunes.

The younger Winthrop was back in England early in 1635 and was busy arranging for live-stock to be sent from Ireland to New England. One of his contacts, Sir John Clotworthy, who though a prominent English settler in Ulster was closely linked with Presbyterian radicals in Ulster and Scotland, was collecting cows, sheep and mares for Winthrop to convey to Massachusetts - evidence that the trade in livestock from Ireland to New England, as well as to Virginia, was now under way. A few men from Ireland had already joined the settlers who were assembling in London to leave for New England with Winthrop.

Livestock was not Clotworthy's main concern. He was deeply involved in a plan to send a substantial contingent of Ulster planters to Massachusetts. He communicated with Winthrop by cipher and told him that a great ship was being built, and that he was anxious that the party should leave as soon as possible, 'so that before the state can send to inhibit, we may have dispatched a competent number'. The ship was slow to come off the stocks at Carrickfergus, and to be equipped. The arrangements to bring a party from Scotland in time to sail, but not to be hampered by appearing too soon, proved complex. (For a note on the Scottish connection, see the Appendix.) John Livingston spoke of 'much toil in our preparations and many hindrances in our setting out.' Meantime, in Ulster, anxious consultations took place as to who should go and who should stay.

The ship was not completed in 1635 after all: for some
reason of which we know nothing she was not ready even
for the easy summer sailing in 1636.   Only in September
1636 was she ready.   She was the *Eaglewing*, 150 tons,
Captain Andrew Agnew, named perhaps in honour of the
flagship of the Winthrop fleet of 1630, the *Arbella* having
been originally named *Eagle*.   The ship left Carrickfergus with
140 passengers on 9 September, a most unfortunate time for
a transatlantic voyage to begin.   The ocean was rough and
treacherous in that season and the passengers began to doubt
if they could make the crossing.   Finally, when, as John
Livingston said long after, 'we were between three and four
hundred leagues from Ireland and so nearer the bank of
Newfoundland than any part of Europe we foregathered with
a mighty hurricane from the north-east'.   The ship's rudder
gave under the strain, but was repaired after heroic and
fortunate efforts by Captain Agnew, yet the wind remained
high.   The ministers aboard, with their strong sense of being
in   communication   with   their   God,   had   (according   to
Livingston) 'thought we had the Lord's warrant for our
intended voyage'.   But the winds were His work, too, and it
seemed to them 'if ever the Lord spake by His winds and
other dispensations, it was made evident to us that it was not
His will that we should go to New England'.   The passengers
were democratically consulted, and all of them agreed with
this reading of the Almighty's intentions.   So it was decided
that the ship should put back and, as Livingston says, 'after
some tossing, we came at last, on third of November to an
anchor in Lochfergus [Belfast Lough]'.   God's verdict, thus
interpreted, was regarded as final, and no attempt was made
to renew the venture either from Ulster or from Scotland.
The Scottish contingent returned home - some of them soon
to take a very prominent part in the national uprising.   The

Ulster Scots also went back to pick up the threads again - not easy for those who had sold their possessions - and to put up with several years of harassment under the Black Oath until they could get their own back at their tormentor, Wentworth, soon created earl of Strafford, in whose impeachment in 1641 Sir John Clotworthy played a prominent part. New England was left to go its own way, unhelped or unhindered by an Ulster contingent.

What hurt Livingston was the shame of failure: 'That which grieved us most was, that we were like to be a mockery to the wicked'. They were closely watched in Ulster, and indeed the departure of the *Eaglewing* was probably regarded with satisfaction by the authorities as removing troublemakers. Bishop Bramhall of Derry wrote on 7 June 1637 to Archbishop Laud that 'the ringleaders of our Nonconformists were all embarked for New England ... [but] ... their faith not being answerable to their zeal they returned and are now in Scotland'. Addressing the Ulster Presbyterians in general he was more scathing still: 'so you, when you are cast out of the Church, are preparing to go and dwell in the Land of Noddies [apparently the Massachusetts Commonwealth was regarded as the abode of idiots], and it is strange if the sides of one ship can contain them, which cannot be kept within the pale of the church'. This curious episode reveals very well the dilemma of the 'Nonconformist' planters in Ireland as compared with the experience of those 'Nonconformists' who went directly from England to America. In New England the latter could and did escape entirely from both civil and ecclesiastical control. In Ulster, where economically the former could do well enough, perhaps very well, they were still within the orbit of the state, subject to its changes of policy in both religious and civil matters.

In some ways it seems a pity, historically, that the emigration from Ulster and from Scotland did not happen, that ill-luck and a curious fatalism wrecked a plan which would earlier have offered a bridge of the sort that bound Ulster to the new United States a century-and-a-half later. Whether the Scots from Ireland and Scotland would have been able to live with the Commonwealthsmen in Massachusetts we do not know. It is plausible that they would have proved too intolerant of one another, yet there were still many parts of New England where they could have lived apart. And since land was available as an economic incentive and a potential common interest, what they shared in religion might eventually have outweighed what they differed on.

VIII. *Irishmen in Brazil, Guiana and the Leeward Islands*

The appearance of Irish settlements on the Amazon in the early seventeenth century appears to have been largely due to the initiative of Philip and James Purcell, two members of an Old English Catholic family, possibly from the Dublin area.[30] Philip traded outward from Dartmouth and took part in a trading voyage to Guiana in 1611, forming an association with Sir Thomas Roe, who was concerned to penetrate deep into the Amazon delta as an area of rich economic potential. Purcell's connections with Ireland remained close and in 1612 he took out fourteen Irishmen to the delta, where they erected a fort and developed a plantation at Taurege on the North Channel. The party formed a free association without indentured labour, so far as can be ascertained, and settled down and prospered between 1612 and 1623, being reinforced in the intervening years by other Irish settlers, possibly some as indentured labourers, so that by the latter year there were at least 70 Irish there, perhaps more. They traded tobacco, dyes and hardwoods, mainly using Dutch shipping. They established close relations with the adjoining Indian groups, who in return for European goods did most of the cultivation and collecting for them. The absence of friction in this region between the Indians on the one hand and the Irish, English and Dutch settlers and traders on the other, appears to have been due, at least in part, to the friendly treatment the Indians received from these Europeans, in contrast to the brutality and intolerance of the Portuguese, who from 1616 onwards were established at Belém on the Atlantic coast. The Irish settlement was Catholic but does not appear to have had any clergy and certainly did not engage in any missionary activity, which the Indians associated with Portuguese coercion.

The settlers remained very healthy, and were indeed the first northern European group to do so in equatorial regions. There were no women or children in the settlement, though there may have been some coming and going to Ireland where female associations and family life were perhaps maintained. In 1620 Roger North took the lead in the new English Amazon Company, in association with Sir Thomas Roe, who in turn was linked with Ricard Burke, earl of Clanricard. It is not unlikely that it was through Burke that North arranged for a further group of Irish settlers to go out to the Amazon under Bernard O'Brien, who claimed to be the son of Connor O'Brien of Leamanagh, County Clare (d.1604), though this is uncertain. The initial group of twelve settlers went out with four English servants and established themselves up-stream from Taurege. The actual site is not known but O'Brien called it *Cocodivae*. Such names of these Irishmen as we have suggest that they were mostly Old English rather than Gaelic in origin. They seem to have established good relations both with Purcell's men at Taurege and with the local peoples. O'Brien apparently explored some way up the Amazon, but unfortunately details are not known. Professor Lorimer suggests that he also crossed overland from the Amazon delta to the Wiapoco River in Guiana. The Dutch West India Company was active in the area from 1621, and because hostilities with Spain and Portugal were renewed in that year the Portuguese reacted sharply to the incursion of Dutch, Irish and English into what they regarded as their territory. In 1623 Pedro Teixeira led a force of Portuguese and Indians against these intruding settlements, several of which were temporarily occupied. The Irish were driven from their base at Taurege, and a number of settlers set sail for the Netherlands. The following year a fresh Dutch expedition was sent out and some Irish under Philip Purcell accompanied it. Taurege was reoccupied, and for a time the Dutch were able to revive trade and settlement on the former basis. But in 1625, Teixeira, with a stronger force, came back to make a clean sweep of all the Amazon settlements. It appears that no fewer than 56 Irish, including Philip Purcell, were killed, after capture by the Portuguese, while the remainder, numbering at least 18, and including James Purcell and Bernard O'Brien, were kept prisoners in the Belém area. Purcell, O'Brien and some others later escaped.

A new English Company was created in 1627 to restore the position in the Amazon. Though most of the English settlers went instead to the Wiapoco River near Guiana, they also revived a post on the Amazon in 1629. However, an Irish contingent travelled out with a Dutch group in 1627, James Purcell, Mathew O'Malley and William Gayner among them, and they revived the Taurege settlement and reverted to their previous trading practices. By this time O'Brien had begun to make overtures to Spain, suggesting that the Catholic Irish should be allowed to remain in the Amazon. Although this gained no response, it became known to the English settlers, who regarded the Irish move as treacherous. The Portuguese renewed their attacks and the English post, along with the revived Irish settlement at Taurege, were both finally overrun in February 1631. This time the Portuguese released the leading men of the Irish group, Gayner in 1633 and O'Brien in 1635. The latter, after going back to the Netherlands, went on to Spain, where he produced an important memorandum on the advantages to Spain of an Irish colony, independent of the English and composed of experienced planters, as a vehicle for the conversion of the Indians. At an earlier date, 1631, an Irish merchant in Spain, known as Jasper Chillan (but thought to have been an O'Brien) had made a similar proposal to the Spanish crown. Bernard O'Brien had however no success, since the Spanish king preferred to allow the Portuguese overseas empire to be administered separately from Spain's and did not intend to intervene in the Amazon. O'Brien finally gave up his Amazon planning in 1636 and left Spain.

Irish participation in successive Guiana enterprises has attracted less published attention but was probably a less significant episode than Irish activities in the Amazon delta.[31] The first English colony on the Wiapoco River was begun in 1604 and survived for little more than a year, but in 1609 Roger Harcourt, an English Catholic, took a substantial colony to settle at Oyapock on the river. This colony contained some Irishmen, but we do not know in what circumstances they joined Harcourt, whether as planters or as servants. The colony lasted until 1612, when it disintegrated owing to a failure to remain on good terms with the local Indians. It was primarily a tobacco venture. When Harcourt left it, a number of the colonists also deserted it and associated themselves with more stable Dutch posts, and among the deserters were some Irish. When Roger North obtained permission to plant colonies in Guiana in 1620 (a privilege soon revoked by James I under Spanish pressure) he found a few Irish survivors of Harcourt's colony, who now joined him at Oyapock on the Wiapoco, since he had some Irishmen in his own company. In 1623 the colony was joined by a few more Irishmen who had escaped from the Portuguese attack on the Amazon settlement. But this Guiana settlement failed through the breakdown of communications with England, and the colonists, again including the Amazon refugees and some other Irish, moved in 1624 to St Christophers, to join Thomas Warner's new colony there.

They were the first of a long series of further Irish arrivals there. We have little information about the status of those who followed the initial planters, but almost all were indentured servants, the assembly and transport of whom remains undocumented, so far as is known to date. The incentive was regular employment in good circumstances (a promise not by any means always honoured) and the award of some land of their own, something they could not hope for in Ireland, at the end of their term. The island had to be shared, almost from the beginning, with French planters, but both groups were expelled by the Spaniards in 1629. Warner soon returned, probably accompanied by some of the original Irish settlers. It was, however, Anthony Hilton of Barnstable who first brought a substantial Irish contingent to St Christophers. He had earlier touched there while on a trading mission to Virginia, presumably in connection with the tobacco trade. On his return he called at an Irish port where he had already had contacts and where 'Captain Wallett [sic] and other gentlemen of Ireland', hearing of St Christophers, 'thought it might be profitable for them to settle a plantation at St Christophers to make tobaccoes'. He returned to

Barnstaple after disposing of his cargo and set out again for Ireland, where 'he was accordingly sett forth by those gentlemen with Shipp and men & all things necessary for the voyage'. It is evident the projectors were going as planters, but they would have had servants with them. No details of the people involved, or even of the port from which they sailed, have come to light. At St Christophers, Warner assigned them to the windward side of the island. This proved too vulnerable to Carib raids and the settlers moved to the leeward side and managed to grow some tobacco, which Hilton took back and sold for them in Ireland. He returned to the Caribbean and, with the settlers, resolved on 22 July 1628 to move to Nevis and establish himself over an Irish colony there. Thus it seems that Nevis became the first essentially Irish colony in the Leeward group, though Hilton's settlers were expelled for a time by the Spaniards in 1629.

Nevis was followed by Montserrat and by Antigua. Nothing is known about the initial establishment of the settlement on Montserrat, other than that it was largely an Irish one. Father Andrew White, on the voyage of the first Maryland settlers in 1634, noted in his journal of their passage through the Caribbean:

[26 January 1634] By noone we came before Monserat, where is a noble plantation of Irish Catholiques whome the Virginians would not suffer to live with them because of their religion.[32]

It might seem that these were the Old English landowners from Waterford ordered to be expelled from Ireland and sent to Virginia in 1630, being then rejected by that colony. But, at a later date, Captain Anthony Briskett, son of Lodwick Briskett, an Anglo-Italian who had been a planter in Ireland in Queen Elizabeth's time, claimed to have been the originator of the plantation, 'to his great costs and charges'. Briskett was subsequently confirmed as governor of the island by the earl of Carlisle, to whom Charles I had granted the Leeward Islands in 1627 and who derived his authority from levies on the settlers there and from the power to confirm the leaders of the island communities as governors under him. Further information appears to be lacking, but presumably Montserrat did continue to flourish as an Old English and New English settlement of Irish origin during subsequent years.

Barbados was the subject of controversy during the later 1620s between various claimants, but organised settlement developed from 1630 onwards. Would-be proprietors rushed to occupy the fertile rim of the island. It is probable that Irish servants were recruited for Barbados well before Thomas Anthony brought out his 'Virginia' servants there in 1637, since Father White noted in January 1634 that in Barbados 'some few Catholiques there be both English and Irish' - whether they were proprietors or servants is not clear.[33] Certainly by 1640 a large number of Irish had come as servants and the fertile rim of the island had become dangerously overcrowded. The same was soon true also of St Christophers, although the claim made in 1643 that there were 22,000 Irish in St. Christophers greatly exaggerated the number.

The Irish, both Old English and Gaelic Irish, obviously played a considerable part in the development of the English Leeward Islands in the period before 1640. However, their position sharply deteriorated shortly after the latter date, as has recently been shown. The causes were primarily the import of African slaves and the consequent downgrading of Irish labour, while sugar cultivation, replacing tobacco, required different skills, skills less directed to cultivation and directed more to manufacture. The growing breach between Irish and English in British politics after 1641 also played a considerable part in the decline of status among both planters and servants from Ireland.[34]

Conclusion

Relations between Ireland and the Americas made a slow start between 1500 and 1600 but developed rapidly between 1600 and 1640. By 1600 only a tiny handful of Irishmen had crossed the wide wastes of the Atlantic and seen American shores. For instance, only a few Catholic clergy and the occasional soldier had lived in North America for more than a few months. But in the years between 1607 and 1640 much of this changed. Irishmen were still few in North America, but numerous at times in the Amazon, Guiana and the Leeward Islands.[35] The Atlantic had become a thoroughfare across which Ireland lay like a stepping stone. Not all the brave ventures succeeded, not all had lasting influence. Irish emigrants to the Amazon and Guiana produced colonies which soon collapsed and disappeared, Irish emigration to the Caribbean was eventually submerged. Lasting Irish influence was to be concentrated in North America, even if success there was partly related to the experience of failure elsewhere. Irish ventures did not always follow in the wake of English ventures but sometimes paralleled them and occasionally preceded them; while often, of course, initiatives and enterprises involved men from both sides of the Irish Sea. Inevitably, however, Irish ventures were drawn, in the end almost exclusively, to the field of England's most successful settlement, in North America.

In 1617 Richard Whitbourne said of Newfoundland that it 'lieth near the course and half the way between Ireland and Virginia'. Fynes Moryson went further and spoke of Ireland as 'this famous Island in the Virginia Sea'. Planters who were making money in Ireland turned their attention also to making money in Virginia. Those who found the power of the Dublin government too near and too inimical looked for refuge to New England's shores. Irish men and women thought of Virginia, like the Caribbean Islands, as a place to labour with some hope of greater reward than they might get at home. There were ideas of linking closely in settlement and in trade the two great islands standing off their respective continents, Ireland and Newfoundland, though only a very few of the great hopes expressed in 1623 were realised. But Irish cattle, Irish sheep, Irish wolfhounds, and Irish victuals, as well as men and women from Ireland, crossed the Atlantic to help to stock the earliest English settlements in North America. None of these things developed as they might have done on account of the great upheavals which began in 1641, but they formed something of a preliminary scenario for what was to take place later, when Ireland was fully locked into the trade system of the North Atlantic and when Scottish planters' descendants and Irish Catholics alike could look to America to better their fortunes and broaden their experience. The later links were first forged before 1640, even if the bond did not, at that time, hold.

APPENDIX

The Scottish Element in the Ulster Emigration Project

The Scottish dimension to the New England emigration project of the Ulster Scots is relevant because there is some evidence that the idea of moving themselves and their congregations to New England originated in Scotland rather than in Ulster, and certainly the Ulster project was followed with sympathy in Scotland.

Professor Gordon Donaldson has drawn attention to the letters of Samuel Rutherford, the Scottish divine, as throwing some light on the course of Scottish interest in New England.[36]   Rutherford wrote as early as 21 July 1630: 'I am credibly informed, that multitudes of England, and especially worthy preachers, and silenced preachers of London, are gone to New England; and I know one learned holy preacher, who hath written against the Arminians, who is gone thither … And now there is such a noise of crying sins in the land … that Christ is putting on His clothes, and making Him, like an ill-handled stranger, to go to other lands.'[37]

How far there had been any moves to plan an emigration to New England between then and 1635 does not appear, but in January in that year John Winthrop the younger attempted to put such a movement in train.   He arrived in Scotland from Antrim bearing letters from John Livingston, who was already in Ireland, to Provost John Stewart in Ayr, David Dickson in Irvine, and James Murray in Edinburgh, which opened up the question.[38]   We know very little about Winthrop's activities in the west of Scotland and in Edinburgh and Leith before he moved on to England in February, but it seems probable that some of those who went to Ulster to plan an American voyage were alerted at this stage. Rutherford wrote on 22 April to Marion McNaught - 'to try your husband afar off, to see if he can be induced to think upon going to America',[39] her husband being William Fullerton, provost of Kirkcudbright. Moreover, Rutherford kept in touch with the venture when it was in preparation, and wrote to Robert Cunningham, minister of Holywood, County Down, on 4 August 1636 - 'I know not, my dear brother, if our worthy brethren be gone to sea or not. They are in my heart and in my prayers. If they be yet with you, salute my dear friend, John Stuart, my well-beloved brethren in the Lord, Mr Blair, Mr Livingston, and Mr McClelland, and acquaint them with my troubles'.[40] In spite, however, of his own difficulties with the ecclesiastical authorities Rutherford did not attempt to join his friends in Ulster.

After hearing of the unfortunate return of the ship, Rutherford wrote to John Kennedy, bailiff of Ayr, on 1 January 1637 - 'My soul is grieved for the success of our brethren's journey to New England; but God hath somewhat to reveal that we see not.'[41] From prison in Aberdeen on 7 February 1637 he wrote also to Robert Blair, now back in Scotland - 'I believe that the Lord tacketh His ship often to fetch the wind, and that He purposeth to bring mercy out of your sufferings and silence'. He sent salutations by Blair to Robert Cunningham and John Livingston, now like Blair in Scotland (along with two Englishmen, clergy also in Ireland but expelled for presbyterian leanings, John Ridge and Henry Colwart).[42] To Livingston himself he wrote the same day: 'I suffer with you in grief, for the dash that your desires to be at New England have received of late; but if our Lord, who hath skill to bring up His children, had not seen it your best, it would not have befallen you ... It is true that Antichrist

stirreth his tail; but I love a rumbling and raging devil in the
kirk ..., rather than a subtle or sleeping devil.'[43]   Later in
the same year, writing to John Stuart, provost of Ayr, he sent
his love to Blair, Livingston and Cunningham, saying - 'Let
me hear from you, for I am anxious what to do.   If I saw
a call for New England, I would follow it'[44]; and in another
undated letter of the same year to Stuart he tells him - 'I am
confident ye shall yet say, that God's mercy blew your sails
back to Ireland again'.[45]   And, indeed, Blair, Livingston,
McClelland and James Hamilton, all in flight from Strafford,
became ministers in Scotland in 1637-8, and played a
significant part in the Scottish events of 1638 and thereafter.

The failure of the *Eaglewing*'s voyage and the consequent
return of the leading members of her complement to Scotland
were regarded by William Row later in the century as
evidence of God's providence.   'But neither the prelates and
conformists, nor they themselves, knew that within a year the
Lord would not only root out the prelates in Scotland, and
after that out of England and Ireland, but make the some of
them, especially Messrs Blair, Livingstone and Maclellan, &c.,
to be very instrumental in the work of reformation.'[46]   The
historian can nod some agreement.   Had the *Eaglewing* carried
off these men to New England, and had they been followed
by other vessels from Scotland, it could well have been that
many of those who led the national uprising in 1638 would
have been absent in North America.

NOTES

1. See D.B. Quinn, 'Atlantic Islands', in J. de Courcy
   Ireland and D.C. Sheehy, *Atlantic visions* (Dublin,
   1989), 77-93.
2. Public Record Office, London [henceforth P.R.O.],
   Bristol Customs Accounts 1503-1504, E122/199, f.3; and
   see Louis-André Vigneras, *The discovery of South
   America and the Andalusian voyages* (Chicago, 1976),
   passim.
3. D.B. Quinn, *England and the discovery of America*
   (London, 1974), 167-70.
4. Alwyn A. Ruddock, 'The reputation of Sebastian Cabot',
   Bulletin of the Institute of Historical Research,
   XLVII (1974), 198.
5. Ada K. Longfield, *Anglo-Irish trade in the sixteenth
   century* (1929), pp.56-7; P.R.O., Bristol Customs
   Account, 1536-7, E122/199, f.22; K.P. Wilson, *Chester
   customs accounts, 1301-1566* (Lancashire and Cheshire
   Record Society, 1969), 89; *Calendar of State Papers,
   Ireland 1574-85*, esp. pp.268,343.
6. John Appleby, 'The fishing ventures of Nicholas Weston
   of Dublin', *Dublin Historical Record*, XXXXIX
   (1986), 150-5.
7. J.G. Shea, *The Catholic Church in colonial days* (4
   vols, New York, 1886-90), 1: 453; Maynard Geiger,
   The Franciscan conquest of Florida, 1573-1618
   (Washington, D.C., 1937), passim; D.B. Quinn, A.M.
   Quinn and S. Hillier, *New American world* (5 vols,
   London/New York, 1979), 5: 128-35.

8. D.B. Quinn, *The Roanoke voyages* (2 vols, Hakluyt Society, Cambridge, 1955), passim; D.B. Quinn, *Set fair for Roanoke* (Chapel Hill, N.C., 1985), 90,275,307.

9. P.E.H. Hair, 'An Irishman before the Mexican Inquisition, 1574-5', *Irish Historical Studies*, XVII (1971), 297-319.

10. Quinn, *England and the discovery of America*, 255-6, n.28; *Set fair for Roanoke*,24,27,42,43,73,237,284; Quinn et al., *New American world*, 3: 329-31.

11. D.B. Quinn, *The Elizabethans and the ̄ Irish* (Ithaca, N.Y., 1966), 120-2.

12. Richard Hakluyt, 'A discourse of western planting [1584]', in E.G.R. Taylor, *The writings and correspondence of the two Richard Hakluyts* (2 vols., Hakluyt Society, London, 1935), 2: 267.

13. Quinn, *England and the discovery of America*, 387-8.

14. D.B. Quinn and A.M. Quinn, *The English New England voyages, 1602-1608* (Hakluyt Society, London, 1981), 242-7, Quinn, *England and the discovery of America*, 383-6.

15. *Ibid.*, 387.

16. D.B. Quinn, 'The voyage of *Triall*, 1606-7', in D.B. Quinn, *Explorers and colonies: America, 1500-1625* (London, 1990), 363-81.

17. For 1607, Aubrey Gwynn, 'The Irish in the West Indies', *Analecta Hibernica*, IV (1932), 159: for 1609, Alexander Brown, *The Genesis of the United States* (2 vols., Boston, 1891), 1: 175; Quinn, *England and the discovery of America*, 392.

18. P.L. Barbour, *The Jamestown voyages under the first charter, 1606-1609* (2 vols., Hakluyt Society, Cambridge, 1969), 1: 157.

19. Michael MacCarthy-Morrogh, *The Munster plantation* (Oxford, 1986), 151,162,174,187, 189,213-14,253,258; S.M. Kingsbury, *Records of the Virginia Company of London* (4 vols, Washington, D.C., 1906-35), 1: 446-7,466,468,472, 2: 482-3, 3: 472, 4: 210.

20. Kingsbury, *Records*, 1: 420,501-2,535,554,562,618,626, 2:65,105,116,210,219,456,497, 643; MacCarthy-Morrogh, *Munster plantation*, 210-13; Carl Bridenbaugh, *Vexed and troubled Englishmen* (2nd ed., New York, 1976), 417: F.W. Gookin, *Daniel Gookin* (Chicago, 1912), 40-50; P.L. Barbour, *The complete works of Captain John Smith* (3 vols., Chapel Hill, N.C., 1986), 2: 72,302-23; R. Beale Davis, *George Sandys* (Charlottesville, 1955), 115,135,151.

21. The fullest account of the Indian rising of March 1622 states that Elizabeth City and Newport News were unaffected and that no casualties occurred, but while they do not appear on official lists it is clear that men were in fact killed at both places. This account of the rising, Frederick J. Fausz, 'The Powhatan rising of 1622', (Ph.D. thesis, College of William and Mary, Williamsburg, Va., 1977), takes the accepted view.

22. Joyce A. Lorimer, *English and Irish settlements on the River Amazon, 1550-1646* (Hakluyt Society, London, 1989), 89,294,391.

23. Gwyn, 'The Irish in the West Indies', 159; George O'Brien, ed., *Advertisements for Ireland* (Royal Society of Antiquaries of Ireland, 1923), 44 - inveighing against the prevalence of beggers in Ireland, it suggests that 'if Virginia or some other of the newly discovered lands in the west were filled with them, it could not but serve and raise the country much, and relieve and advance

them withal!' (the date is about 1623, the author probably Sir Arthur Bourgchier).

24. T.W. Moody et al., *A new history of Ireland, 3*, (Oxford, 1976), 601.

25. MacCarthy-Morrogh, *Munster plantation*, 211-13; A.E. Smith, *Colonists in bondage* (Chapel Hill, N.C., 1947), 61-6, using P.R.O., High Court of Admiralty, HCA30/636; Carl and Roberta Bridenbaugh, *No Peace beyond the Line. The English in the Caribbean, 1624-1690* (New York, 1972), 14-15; also see K.R. Andrews, *Ships, money and politics: seafaring and naval enterprise in the reign of Charles I* (Cambridge, 1991).

26. The Irish part is well represented in Gillian T. Cell, *English enterprise in Newfoundland, 1577-1660* (Toronto, 1969), and her documentary collection, *Newfoundland discovered. English attempts at colonization 1610-1630* (Hakluyt Society, London, 1982), which reprints the rare 1623 Dublin pamphlet (227-37). See also Luca Codignola, *The coldest harbour of the land. Simon Stock and Lord Baltimore's colony in the land, 1621-1640* (Kingston, Ont., 1988).

27. No Old English or Gaelic Irish names have been identified in lists of the earliest settlers in Maryland, where Jesuit priests were present from the beginning: G. Skordas, *The early settlers of Maryland* (Annapolis, Md., 1974). But it is probable that, even if there were no freemen from Ireland among the settlers, there were at least some Irish among the indentured servants, whose names were not normally recorded.

28. J.K. Hosmer, *Winthrop's journal, 1630-1649* (2 vols, New York, 1908), 1: 127; A.B. Forbes et al, *Winthrop papers* (6 vols, Cambridge, Mass., 1929-), vol.2, passim.
29. The Ulster planters' project is covered in 'The life of Mr. John Livingston', in W.K. Guthrie, *Select biographies* (Wodrow Society, Edinburgh, 1845), 1: 148-56; Patrick Adair, *A true narrative of the rise and progress of the Presbyterian church in Ireland* (Belfast, 1866), 40-8; J.S. Reid, *History of the Presbyterian church in Ireland* (4 vols, Belfast, 1867), 1: 89,96-8,106-10,119-28,195.
30. Lorimer, *English and Irish settlements on the River Amazon*, 40-101. This volume transforms our previous knowledge of Irish activity in the region.
31. The authorities for the appearance of the Irish (and English) in Guiana are James A. Williamson, *English colonies in Guiana and on the Amazon* (Oxford, 1923); Vincent T. Harlow, *Colonising expeditions to the West Indies and Guiana 1623-67* (Hakluyt Society, London, 1925); and Gwynn, 'Irish in the West Indies'. See especially Harlow, lxx-lxxix, 5,13,15,19; Gwynn, 'The Irish in the West Indies', 153-6,169-71; and see also Bridenbaugh, *No Peace beyond the Line*, 14-15,20 n.18. When Joyce Lorimer's Ph.D. thesis, 'English trade and exploration in Trinidad and Guiana, 1569-1648' (Liverpool, 1974), is published a much clearer picture will emerge.
32. Clayton C. Hall, *Narratives of early Maryland, 1633-84* (New York, 1910), 38.
33. Ibid., 37.

34. See Hilary McD. Beckles, 'A "riotous and unruly lot"; Irish indentured servants and freemen in the English West Indies, 1644-1713', *William and Mary Quarterly*, XLVII (1990), 503-22. He says that in the years 1638-1641 'Irish laborers held clear preferences for certain islands', presumably St Christophers, Nevis and Montserrat, and possibly also Antigua.

35. The economic and political circumstances under which men, and some women too, left Ireland for the Americas in the first forty years of the seventeenth century clearly require further investigation, such as that recently given to the Amazon settlements by Professor Lorimer. The present account is necessarily somewhat superficial as the materials so far available are sparse and comparatively little has been done to study the issue in detail.

36. G. Donaldson, 'The emergence of Schism in seventeenth-century Scotland', *Studies in Church History*, IX (1972), 283-4. I am grateful to Professor Donaldson for bringing Rutherford's *Letters* to my attention and for other assistance.

37. Samuel Rutherford, *Letters*, ed. Andrew A. Bonar, (2 vols, Edinburgh, 1863), 1: 63-4.

38. *Winthrop papers*, 5: 185.

39. Rutherford, *Letters*, 1: 145.

40. *Ibid.*, 170-1.

41. *Ibid.*, 194.

42. *Ibid.*, 232-4.

43. *Ibid.*, 229,232.

44. *Ibid.*, 376.

45. *Ibid.*, 379.

46. William Row 'Supplement', in T.McCrie, *Life of Robert Blair* (Wodrow Society, Edinburgh, 1848), 46.

IRELAND, c. 1600, by K.M. Davies

From T.W. Moody, F.X. Martin and F.J. Byrne (eds.), *A New History of Ireland*, Vol. III: *Early Modern Ireland, 1534-1691*, 1976, p. 144, by Permission of Oxford University Press.

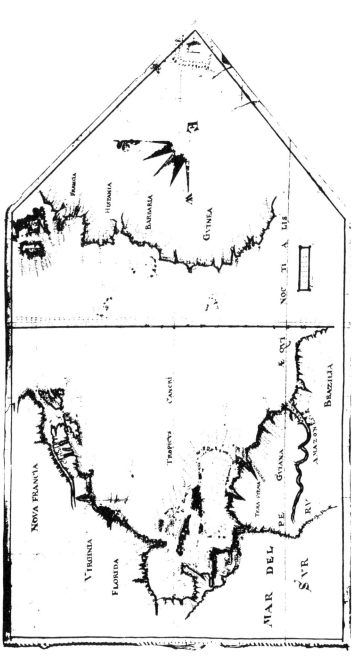

THE ATLANTIC WORLD

[The Virginia Company Chart]. Manuscript map, drawn in gold and colours on vellum. c. 1606-1608 (Stokes c. 1606-1608 C-8). I. N. Phelps Stokes Collection, Miriam and Ira D. Wallach Division of Art, Prints and Photographs, The New York Public Library; Astor, Lennox and Tilden Foundations.